ELOISE CARLSON

Short Stories of a VETERINARIAN

Short Stories of a Veterinarian

Copyright © 2018 Eloise Carlson

Illustration Copyright © 2018 McKay Fife

All rights reserved.

The stories collected in this book are based on true events. Some names and identifying details have been changed to protect the privacy of individuals.

No part of this book may be reproduced or transmitted in any form or by any means, electronic or mechanical, including photocopying, recording, or by any information storage and retrieval system without express written permission from the author.

Hardback Edition

ISBN-13: 978-1-939993-80-9
ISBN-10: 1-939993-80-6

Dedication

Doctor Bob was my father-in-law. Through the years I loved listening to the crazy things that would happen to him as a Veterinarian. I never tired hearing the stories he would tell. After his death I found some diary entrees of these particular stories. I laughed when I read them and then thought, "you need to keep these for the grandchildren and great grandchildren!" I am hoping by giving just a little insight to their grandfather (great grandfather) they will come to know him just a little bit.

So I am happily dedicating this work to him, hope you like them, Dad!

Contents

1: Out of School, Out of Luck 1

2: Tears of Joy 6

3: A Funny Thing Happened 13

4: Rosie 19

About the Author 26

Other Books by Elosie Carlson 28

Introduction

Bob was known to all as a kind, fun-loving, compassionate, and very intelligent person. He was one who never got too upset about anything. He took life's challenges in stride and moved forward. His parents were the first generation in his family to be born in the United States. Prior to his parents, everyone had come from Sweden.

Bob grew up on a farm in California during the Great Depression. He worked alongside his father and learned to work hard. They milked cows and tended to fields full of produce. The milk, tomatoes and watermelon produced on their farm helped the community. Bob's family was not wealthy, but they got along just fine during those tough times.

Bob's reputation as a hard worker paid off throughout his life. He received an athletic scholarship to play football for the University of Iowa. He then served in the Navy during World War II, and when he returned to school, he received another scholarship to play football for the University of Washington.

It was clear that football was important to Bob; but it also became clear that when you are studying to become a veterinarian, you don't have time for football anymore.

This is when he began life as Bob the Vet!

Short Stories of a VETERINARIAN

Out of School, Out of Luck?

Bob walked out of the University of Washington for the last time knowing he had done it! After years in the Veterinarian School of Medicine, he was now a doctor. He had finished as a married student, with extra responsibilities, so this had not been an easy accomplishment. The addition of a new little son really made life interesting. But he had done it! *They* had done it! Bob was full of excitement and ready to go!

He was grateful for the support of his small family, his parents and friends, and he didn't want to let any of them down. He was a new Doctor of Medicine for Animals, and he knew it was time for him to get going. No time to dillydally, no time for vacations, just time for work!

Bob loved all animals and had a special bond with them, almost like he could speak their language. Even the most upset animal could be calmed by his touch. He was eager to use his training now, and his mind raced as he contemplated where his first job might be.

He had grand ideas about what his future practice would look like. Perhaps he really could have an office of his own. Most likely, however, he would join an established practice for a while. Where would he go? What would he do? The sky is the limit, right?

Dr. Bob began working with an older, experienced veterinarian. Dr. Steve was an old timer set in his ways, unwilling to make changes, and quite difficult to work with. Some might even say he was cantankerous. Still, Bob was anxious to learn all he could from the vintage vet, and maybe even become his friend.

Their practice was located in Squim, Washington, near Seattle. Bob traveled from place to place in the farmlands to visit and treat animals that could not be brought into an office. He carried his supplies in the back of his truck and, on his own, he diagnosed health problems that arose. This was not exactly his vision of a corner office with a view.

However, there were still beautiful views where he worked. Bob covered a lot of territory and enjoyed the majestic scenes in the area. He became a good friend to ranchers all around the state.

Dr. Bob was still "wet behind the ears" when he was off on a call and discovered a very serious problem. Ranchers' cattle were dying, dropping like flies. Dr. Steve had a theory of what was causing these deaths, but Dr. Bob was not sure he agreed. He went to get a firsthand look at the cattle, took some blood samples and started to formulate his thoughts about the situation.

Dr. Bob was very systematic in his approach. One by one, he ruled out symptoms that might—or might not—be causing problems with the cattle. He returned to his home base to collaborate with Dr. Steve, telling him that he thought the illness was something called "Bubonic Plague."

The old doctor responded with a look of disgust and said, "We've never had that problem here before. No one has seen that disease in years. You new doctors just out of school think you can read a few books and know what's wrong."

Dr. Bob still felt it would be a good idea to send the blood samples off to the lab at Washington State University, to see what more they could learn. A lot was riding on the results of this test, including his reputation for being able to diagnose properly. The health of the livestock and the livelihood of the ranchers were also in peril.

The lab results verified Bob's diagnosis; it was indeed Bubonic Plague. Dr. Steve was more than happy to be proven wrong, even by a newly-graduated college student. The doctors were then able to inoculate the herds and avoid what could have been a disaster.

Comprehensive Questions

Out of School, Out of Luck?

1. What was The Great Depression?

2. The story talked about a vintage Vet. What does that mean?

3. What is Bubonic Plague? How does it spread?

4. What are you, if you are "wet behind the ears?"

5. What would you say was the relationship between the two doctors?

Tears of Joy

A beautiful day, not a cloud in the sky. Dr. Bob had already made his rounds before going to work, first to feed his horses and then his trusty hunting dog, Trixy. Trixy was a white and yellow dog with one blue eye and one brown eye. Everyone in the family loved her, but Trixy was most loyal to Dr. Bob.

Dr. Bob's animal clinic was right next door to the family home. This made it easy for him to go back and forth to check on an animal's wellbeing. He had built the clinic himself, a dream come true. Now he had his own practice and could treat any animal he wanted to treat—not just horses, not just small animals.

However, this clinic would mostly treat small animals. It did have ample runs in the back if he boarded large dogs. For the most part, the clinic was just what Dr. Bob wanted. He was also the veterinarian for the racetrack, which was great, because horses were probably one of his favorite animals.

On a day that started out as any other day, Dr. Bob checked on all the animals that had undergone surgery the day before. He then reviewed all the upcoming procedures that were to be done. He glanced into the waiting area and saw that the room was full of people and their animals. Dr. Bob loved people and he loved their animals.

He told his receptionist, Jean, to bring the first client in. The dog was yelping in pain. His owner said he wouldn't put any weight on his front paw and it seemed to be swollen. The doc took one look and knew exactly what the problem was.

At that particular time of year, the cheat grass was growing all around. The dog had gotten some cheat grass in his paw and was unable to lick it out. Consequently, the paw became terribly infected.

Dr. Bob called Jean in to assist, and they were able to give the dog a numbing shot in his paw. Now the doctor could make a cut and remove the grass. The only thing left to do was bandage him up and let the healing process begin. One patient down and just eight more to go.

It was a good day, nothing really out of the ordinary to deal with. The last visit of the day, however, was different.

An older couple brought their dog to see Dr. Bob. The dog had been their pride and joy for many years, but now it seemed he was having difficulties with his vision. As the doctor examined the dog, he discovered there were problems, serious problems. The dog was going blind.

Dr. Bob said, "Sometimes a dog this age will have his eye ducts shrivel or dry up."

The couple was devastated and wondered what would happen to their beloved pet. Dr. Bob told them there was really nothing that could be done for him, but then added, "Give me some time to think about the problem, and come back tomorrow."

When Dr. Bob went home that night, he couldn't quite thinking about the dog. He continued to consider all the options. He looked up medical procedures that might improve the dog's eyesight. He pondered on everything he read; and then an idea came to him.

When the couple came back for a consultation the next day, Dr. Bob told them he had been studying into the wee hours of the morning about their dog and his condition. There was really nothing in the medical books that gave any hope for this type of eye problem; and then he said, "Okay, I have a crazy idea that just might work. It has never been done before, but I don't see why it wouldn't work. If you'll let me try, I think I can help your dog's eyesight return."

Dr. Bob explained that he wanted to move the dog's salivary gland and reroute it to the dog's tear ducts, so that anytime the dog saw food, his eyes would water, just as the salivary glands make water in your mouth when you eat. This would keep the dog's eyes hydrated and his vision should improve.

The couple was overjoyed to have some hope, and they were willing to let Dr. Bob do anything he thought was safe and might help. They gave their permission for him to try this unusual procedure; and so, it was done.

A week or so later, the couple returned to the animal clinic. They were happy, and the dog was walking with his head held high. They all seemed to be doing well, and Dr. Bob invited them into his office. They said, "We want to show you something." They put a bowl of food down in front of the dog. "Watch," they said.

As the dog ate his food, he cried like a baby. His eyes were hydrating. He could see better, and the entire family was so happy! They expressed their gratitude to Dr. Bob for saving their dog's eyes.

It is days like these that truly make practicing animal husbandry worth it!

Comprehensive Questions

Tears of Joy

1. What was wrong with the first dog that visited the clinic that day? He had a swollen paw.

2. What was wrong with the older dog that was going blind?

3. What did Doctor Bob do to correct his blindness?

4. What would the dog do when he ate his food?

5. What is animal husbandry?

A Funny Thing Happened

Jessie Wake was an interesting person. She was a sweet lady in her 60's, a practical nurse, housekeeper, cook, and a companion for an elderly man whose last name is Moore.

Mr. Moore was quite the banker in his day. He loved details and having things done in just the right way. But at more than 90 years old, he needed Jessie's help on a daily basis. Jessie was a happy person who seemed to enjoy taking care of Mr. Moore. Aside from all the housekeeping and physical needs he required, she sat to read to him and visit with him. Jessie was a good friend.

Along with caring for Mr. Moore, Jessie took care of the love of her life, an old red tabby cat named. "Joseph" Jessie and Joseph had been friends forever, and Jessie's life revolved around him. Mr. Moore also grew to love the old cat.

Unfortunately, Joey had some health problems, and quite often Jessie would have to take him to the animal hospital to see Dr. Bob. Apparently, Joey produced bladder stones inside his body, and by the time Jessie realized there was a problem, Joseph was in serious trouble. This condition went on for quite a long time.

One evening, Joseph was brought into the clinic in pretty bad shape. He was depressed and dehydrated; his temperature was below normal. He had a terrible odor and was crying out in pain. His vitals were not good, and neither was the prognosis.

Dr. Bob told Jessie he would do the best he could do, and time would tell. The cat needed a catheter first to get fluids going, and Bob started all the necessary procedures; but he worried that it might not be enough. Dr. Bob told Jessie she would have to leave the cat in his care. Jessie didn't want to leave him but knew it would be his only chance.

The doctor worked with the cat through the night; but in the wee hours of the morning, Joseph passed away. Bob waited until midmorning to call Jessie and give her the news. It didn't go so well.

"Jessie, I don't have good news." She began to sob over the phone, and Bob tried to find the right words to soften the hurt. He didn't want her to hold out hope for a possible recovery and told her that Joseph had passed away.

Jessie was so upset and having such a hard time that Bob didn't want to ask any questions about what she wanted to do next. Finally, he told Jessie he would keep Joey until she had decided what she wanted to do with his remains. After their phone conversation ended, even Bob had to sit down for a minute to regain his composure.

But the story gets better.

Mr. Moore had two good friends who looked out for his best interests: a chiropractor by the name of Dr. White, and an attorney by the name of Mr. Hamilton; both men were connected to Mr. Moore's legal affairs.

After Jessie was absent for a day from caring for Mr. Moore, she knew she should call these men to tell them why. When she finally gained her composure enough to talk, she blurted out, "Dr. White, it finally happened!" She began crying again; she was inconsolable and not able to say anything else.

Dr. White immediately thought of his friend Mr. Moore and urgently asked, "What happened? What happened?" He finally settled Jessie down enough to get one short sentence out of her."

"He passed away," she sobbed.

Dr. White tried to calm her and comfort her. He tried to share reassuring thoughts about what to do next, a burial or cremation, which only seemed to make her more upset.

Finally, Jessie cried, "He was all I had!" More sobs and distress. "I can't live without him! Do you think people would think we were terrible if we just had him stuffed and kept him in the living room?"

Dr. White was shocked, and speechless. He finally got off the phone, composed himself and called Mr. Hamilton, the attorney. "You can't imagine what has happened."

Mr. Hamilton responded, "What's happened?"

"Mr. Moore has died."

Mr. Moore? How do you know?"

"Jessie just called and could hardly talk, so I'm not sure about the details. If you can imagine this, she wants to know if she can stuff him and keep him in his chair in the living room."

Mr. Hamilton was incredulous. "What? Do the authorities know?"

"I have no idea."

Mr. Hamilton said, "I think I should go over and see what's going on."

"A good idea," Dr. White agreed.

About thirty minutes later, Mr. Hamilton called and said, "Do you know who died? JESSIE'S CAT!" Let's just say the men were quite relieved.

Comprehensive Questions

A Funny Thing Happened

1. What was Jessie Wake's job?

2. What did Mr. Moore's do for a living?

3. What was the cat's name? Why did she refer to him as Joey occasionally?

4. Who was Dr. White and Mr. Hamilton? What did they do for Mr. Moore?

5. Who died in the story?

4

Rosie

It was about closing time at the clinic, on what had been a fairly uneventful day, with only the usual vaccinations and ear infections. However, as the last client walked in, it looked like things were about to get exciting.

A good friend by the name of Walt Jones came in with a little companion holding his hand. This companion's name was Rosie, and she was the cutest chimpanzee Dr. Bob had ever seen. She was wearing a dress and panties; her outfit included a hat that had a flower on top. She walked right up to Dr. Bob, hugged his leg and looked right up into his eyes.

Dr. Bob said, "Walt, where in the world did you get her?"

"Well, Doc, it's like this. I need some help! On the way home today, I stopped at the Crescent Bar for a drink. Two truck drivers came in and we all started to drink together. We kept talking and drinking, until somehow along the way, I became the proud new owner of this chimp!"

"Oh, man…" said Dr. Bob. "Did you actually buy Rosie? What happened next?"

"Well, everything went pretty well until I got home. I kinda thought my wife and family would like to have a chimpanzee. When Rosie and I walked into the house, my wife took one look at her and said, 'What do you plan to do with that animal?' Well, the way she said it, I could tell that my new friend was not a good idea. The ultimatum was, 'It's either Rosie or me!'"

"Walt, that's a crazy story. What do you want me to do?"

Walt then explained that his two new trucker friends were headed to Seattle to drop off their load and then they would be coming back through town in a week. "Bob, you've got to help me. Can Rosie stay here with you for a week? It'll save my marriage."

"Sure," Dr. Bob said. "I can do that; she can stay here in the clinic, so I don't think my marriage would be in jeopardy" They both had a good laugh at that, and Bob added, "Maybe this is just what you need to quit drinking."

Bob's family had a great time with Rosie all week. Everyone loved her, and she treated them well in return. Bob would take her to the house and the kids all took turns holding her and playing with her. She especially liked it when they carried her around. Not too many kids get to play with a chimpanzee.

It didn't take long to discover that Rosie could get the family to do anything she wanted. She only weighed 70 pounds, and Bob weighed about 210 pounds; but there was no question about who was the stronger of the two. It wasn't Bob.

Rosie stayed with Bob and his family for just that week, but they will never forget her. It was quite an adventure to share some playtime with a cute, well-dressed chimpanzee.

Bob often wondered how many times those truckers helped their financial status with this little scheme.

Comprehensive Questions

Rosie

1. Who was Walt Jones and what did he bring into the clinic?

2. Who was Rosie?

3. How much did Rosie weigh?

4. Where did she stay for a week?

5. What kind of clothes did Rosie wear?

Acknowledgments

I would like to thank McKay Fife for illustrating this book. The type of art he used is a bit different for him and I think it looks great! Also, thank you to Eileen Petersen for editing these short stories for me. Always and forever an appreciation to my husband for his support.

A Note from the Author

Dear Reader,

If you are not familiar with my previous books, it was one of my main goals to included my grandchildren's names somehow in the stories.

With *Mother Did You Kill The Cow,* my first book, I acknowledged my sweet grand kids in the dedication. I wanted each of them to see their names written in my book. Then subsequent books contain additional grandchildren's names as they come along.

In this particular book, Joseph was the grandchild that was mentioned. Now almost 1 1/2 old. I hope I can write many more books.

-Eloise

About the Author

Eloise Beal Carlson is a graduate from Brigham Young University in Early Childhood Education. Marrying her high school sweetheart, her education served her well in rearing their eight children. Eloise enjoys the out of doors, painting, traveling, biking, doing projects with her husband and playing with her grand-children. Storytelling has always been a part of her life.

About the Illustrator

McKay Fife has been drawing since he figured out how to hold a pencil. He is a talented artist, musician, and actor, performing in local theater with lead musical acting roles. He is involved in church activities and scouting. He plays the piano and clarinet, and anything else he can get his hands on! In his spare time, he loves to play video games like *Legend of Zelda* and *Super Mario* and of course, READ.

Other Books by Eloise Carlson

Mother, Did You Kill the Cow?

•

The Tree with the Heart

•

The Sick Little Dinosaur

www.ingramcontent.com/pod-product-compliance
Lightning Source LLC
Chambersburg PA
CBHW070039230426
43661CB00034B/1433/J